Chien-Shiung

PHYSICIST

by Meg Gaertner

FOCUS READERS

READERS

BEACON

www.focusreaders.com

Focus Readers is distributed by North Star Editions:
sales@northstareditions.com | 888-417-0195

Produced for Focus Readers by Red Line Editorial.

Photographs ©: Photo Researchers/Science History Images/Alamy, cover, 1, 4, 16, 22, 29; Shutterstock Images, 7, 8, 11, 12, 14–15, 25; Science History Images/Alamy, 19; AP Images, 21, 26

Library of Congress Cataloging-in-Publication Data
Names: Gaertner, Meg, author.
Title: Chien-shiung Wu : physicist / by Meg Gaertner.
Description: Lake Elmo, MN : Focus Readers, [2021] | Series: Important
    women | Includes index. | Audience: Grades 4-6
Identifiers: LCCN 2020040888 (print) | LCCN 2020040889 (ebook) | ISBN
    9781644936931 (hardcover) | ISBN 9781644937297 (paperback) | ISBN
    9781644938010 (pdf) | ISBN 9781644937655 (ebook)
Subjects: LCSH: Wu, C. S. (Chien-shiung), 1912-1997--Juvenile literature. |
    Chinese American women--Biography--Juvenile literature. |
    Physicists--United States--Biography--Juvenile literature. | Women
    physicists--United States--Biography--Juvenile literature.
Classification: LCC QC16.W785 G34 2021 (print) | LCC QC16.W785 (ebook) |
    DDC 530.092 [B]--dc23
LC record available at https://lccn.loc.gov/2020040888
LC ebook record available at https://lccn.loc.gov/2020040889

Printed in the United States of America
Mankato, MN
012021

About the Author

Meg Gaertner is a children's book editor and writer. She lives in Minneapolis, where she enjoys swing dancing and spending time outside. She is grateful for the opportunities she has, and for the important women whose groundbreaking work made those opportunities possible.

Table of Contents

Chapter 1

Wu's Experiment

Chien-Shiung Wu was a **physicist**. In 1956, she did an experiment. She saw what happened when **atoms** broke apart. One popular idea said that **particles** would fly off in all directions equally.

Like many scientists, Chien-Shiung Wu used experiments to learn about the world.

But that's not what happened. Wu's test showed that the idea was incorrect.

Scientists come up with ideas about how the world works. Then they test those ideas. Sometimes, the ideas are right. Other times, the ideas need to be changed.

Did You Know?

Atoms are made of particles. Some particles stick together. Others move around the rest.

INSIDE AN ATOM

In her work, Wu focused on the particles of the nucleus. She studied how those particles stay together.

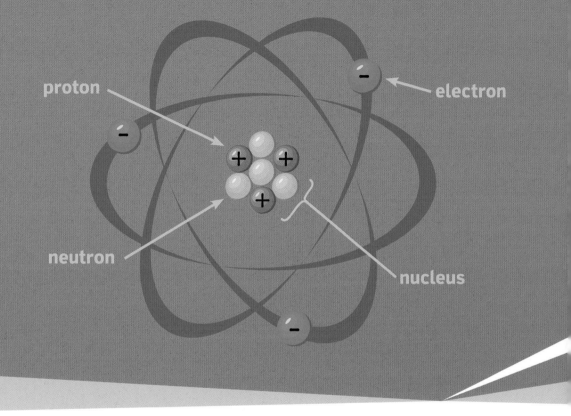

proton

electron

neutron

nucleus

Wu's test changed how scientists saw the world. And it was just one of her discoveries. For her work, Wu is called the "First Lady of **Physics**."

Chapter 2

Becoming a Scientist

Chien-Shiung Wu was born on May 31, 1912. She grew up near Shanghai, China. At the time, it was uncommon for girls to go to school. But Chien-Shiung's parents supported girls' education.

Wu graduated from the National Central University in 1934. The school was later renamed Nanjing University.

Her mother was a teacher. Her father opened one of the first girls' schools in China. Chien-Shiung went to his school.

She read about women in science. Their successes inspired her. She wanted to be a leader in science, too. So, Wu studied physics in

Did You Know?

Marie Curie was a physicist. Her work won many awards. It inspired Wu to study physics.

> **Marie Curie (right) did some of the first research on X-rays.**

college. In 1936, she moved to the United States. She worked with famous scientists in California.

A few years later, World War II (1939–1945) began. Japan attacked the United States in 1941. After this attack, many Asian Americans faced more **racism**. As a result, Wu struggled to find work in California. So, she moved to the East Coast.

Wu taught at several colleges. Then she joined the war effort. She helped make fuel for **atomic bombs**. Her work helped end the war.

After the war, Wu returned to teaching. She taught physics at Columbia University. And she became a US citizen in 1954.

Did You Know?

Wu is thought to be the only Chinese person who worked on the atomic bombs.

The Manhattan Project

During World War II, the US Army had a secret program. It was called the Manhattan Project. Many scientists worked together. They created the first atomic bombs.

Wu joined in 1944. She focused on fuel. Splitting atoms gives off energy. Certain atoms work best. Wu found ways to get large amounts of them. This fuel made the bombs extremely powerful. In 1945, the United States dropped two atomic bombs on Japan. The bombs helped end the war. But they killed more than 100,000 people. So, they have not been used in war again.

Atomic bombs create huge clouds when they explode.

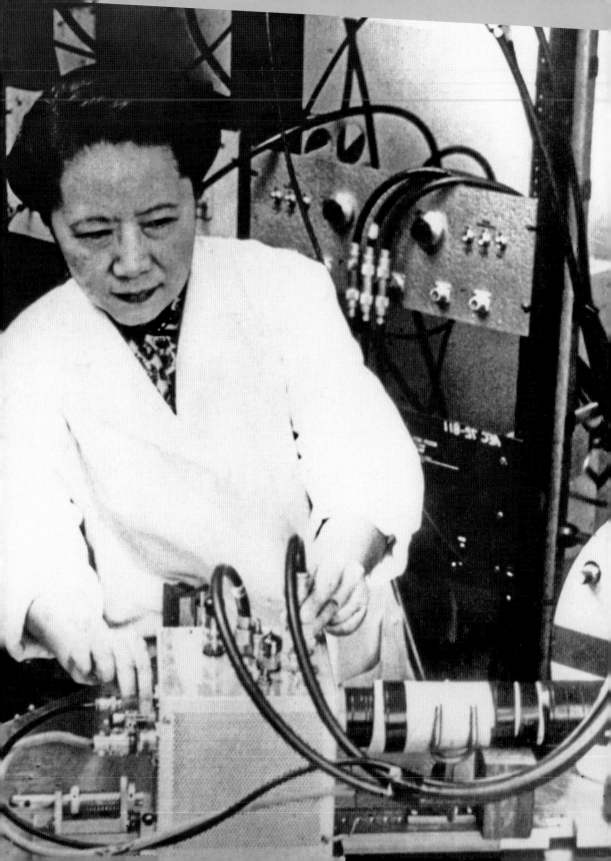

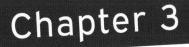
In the Lab

Some physicists think about the world. They develop ideas to explain how it works. Other physicists test those ideas. They do experiments. They work in labs.

Wu's experiments focused on very small particles and how they behaved.

Wu was good at coming up with ways to test ideas. She proved or disproved other people's thoughts. For example, one popular idea explained how particles change. Wu tested the idea. She proved for the first time that it was correct.

In 1956, two scientists had a new idea. At the time, most people believed **identical** particles acted the same. The scientists thought this might not always be true. They asked Wu to test their idea.

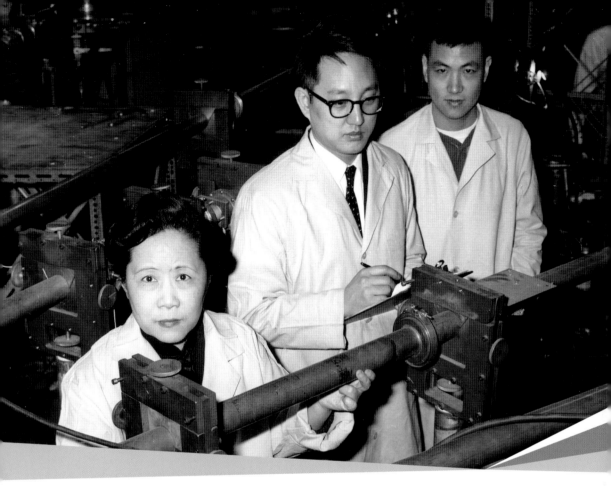

 Wu and her assistants do an experiment at Columbia University in 1963.

Wu agreed. She made a test. It proved the scientists were correct. Wu's test was the most important finding in physics at the time.

It had overturned a **law** of physics. However, Wu did not get much attention for her work.

In 1957, the two scientists won the Nobel Prize in Physics. This prize is a major award. It is given to people who make the biggest discoveries. The men were honored for their idea. Wu had been the

Did You Know?

Wu wrote a book about her research in 1965. Physicists still use it today.

> Dr. Chen Ning Yang (left) and Dr. Tsung-Dao Lee (middle) won the Nobel Prize in 1957.

one to prove it. This is a key step in science. But she was left out of the award.

Chapter 4

Leading the Way

Wu continued to do tests. In 1958, scientists had an idea about particles' movements. Wu proved it in 1963. She tested other ideas as well. She also taught at Columbia until 1981.

 Throughout her long career, Wu made many important discoveries.

Wu's work changed physics. She changed how scientists understood the world. They had to let go of long-held beliefs.

Wu thought it was important to doubt ideas until they had been proved. For Wu, doubt was what pushed science forward.

Did You Know?

Wu is best known for her work in physics. But she also did research in biology and medicine.

> Wu was one of the first women hired at Princeton. At the time, it was still an all-male school.

Wu often faced **sexism**. She did not always receive the same pay as men. And men sometimes received honors for her work.

She also faced racism. But she did not let these barriers stop her.

Wu stayed curious. She followed her love of physics. And she encouraged other women to work in the sciences.

People eventually honored Wu for her work. She received many science awards. In some cases, she was the first woman to receive those awards. Wu also served as president of a top physics organization. She was the first woman in this role.

Wu died on February 16, 1997. People remember her as one of the world's top physicists.

Did You Know?

Wu was buried in China. Her ashes are near the school her father founded.

FOCUS ON
Chien-Shiung Wu

Write your answers on a separate piece of paper.

1. Write a sentence summarizing Wu's impact on physics.

2. If you were a physicist, would you rather come up with ideas or test ideas? Why?

3. When did Wu move to the United States?
- A. 1936
- B. 1939
- C. 1945

4. Why might Wu have been overlooked for the 1957 Nobel Prize in Physics?
- A. She had never tested an idea.
- B. She was Chinese and a woman.
- C. Her test was not important.

5. What does **disproved** mean in this book?

*Wu was good at coming up with ways to test ideas. She proved or **disproved** other people's thoughts.*

    A. showed that something is correct

    B. showed that something is incorrect

    C. asked for more information

6. What does **barriers** mean in this book?

*She also faced racism. But she did not let these **barriers** stop her.*

    A. things that help people in their work

    B. ideas that can be tested

    C. things that get in someone's way

Answer key on page 32.

Glossary

atomic bombs
Powerful weapons that create explosions by splitting atoms.

atoms
The smallest building blocks of matter. They make up everything in the physical world.

identical
Exactly alike in every way.

law
In science, a widely held idea that explains how the world works. Laws are supported by experiments and by what scientists see in the world.

particles
Tiny bits that make up atoms.

physicist
A scientist who studies physics.

physics
The study of matter and how it moves and acts.

racism
Hatred or mistreatment of people because of their skin color or ethnicity.

sexism
Hatred or mistreatment of people because of their gender.

To Learn More

BOOKS

Bodden, Valerie. *Nuclear Physicist Chien-Shiung Wu*. Minneapolis: Lerner Publications, 2017.

Doeden, Matt. *The Manhattan Project*. Minneapolis: Lerner Publications, 2019.

Robeson, Teresa. *Queen of Physics: How Wu Chien Shiung Helped Unlock the Secrets of the Atom*. New York: Sterling Children's Books, 2019.

NOTE TO EDUCATORS

Visit **www.focusreaders.com** to find lesson plans, activities, links, and other resources related to this title.

Index

A
atomic bombs, 13, 14
atoms, 5–7, 14

C
Columbia University,
    13, 23
Curie, Marie, 10

E
experiments, 5, 17

M
Manhattan Project, 14

N
Nobel Prize in Physics, 20

P
particles, 5–7, 18, 23
physics, 7, 10, 13, 19–20,
    24, 26–27

T
testing, 6–7, 17–19, 23

W
World War II, 12–13, 14